R O B E R T   B U R T O N

KW-054-564

ANIMAL HOMES

TOWNS

photographs by Oxford Scientific Films

❦ Belitha Press

First published in Great Britain in 1991 by
Belitha Press Limited
31 Newington Green, London N16 9PU
Text copyright © Robert Burton 1991
Photographs copyright © Oxford Scientific
Films and individual copyright holders 1991
All rights reserved. No part of this book may
be reproduced or utilized in any form or by any
means, electronic or mechanical, including
photocopying, recording or by any information
storage and retrieval system, without
permission in writing from the Publisher.
Printed in Singapore for Imago Publishing

ISBN 1 85561 045 0

British Library Cataloguing in Publication Data
CIP data for this book is available from the British Library

The publishers wish to thank the following for permission
to reproduce copyright material:

Oxford Scientific Films and individual copyright
holders on the following pages: Kathie Atkinson 7, Mike
Birkhead 16, 20, Waina Cheng 21, Densey Clyne 22, 23,
Mantis Wildlife/Densey Clyne title page, Jack Dermid 19,
Jim Frazier 9, Terry Heathcote 15, Rodger Jackman 2,
Animals Animals/Breck P. Kent 4, Jos Korenromp 17,
Neil Lathan 10, Michael Leach 3, 6, 10 inset, Animals
Animals/Patty Murray 14, Owen Newman 13, C. M.
Perrins 5, Press-Tige pictures 8, Wendy Shattil/Bob
Rozinski front cover, Alistair Shay back cover, David
Thompson 12, Barry Walker 18

577.8
590

EARDISLEY SCHOOL LIBRARY

01089

Some animals prefer to live in the countryside and rarely come into houses or gardens. Others prefer to live in towns and are rarely found in the country.

House mice are very common in buildings. Many house mice spend their whole lives indoors. Some even live deep under ground in mines and in underground railway stations. They eat food that people have thrown away.

House mice got to North America and Australia by hiding in ships carrying cargoes of grain and other foods. House mice have even reached the frozen land of Antarctica, where they grow thick fur and live in warm nests.

House mice have babies all the year. One female mouse can have five to ten **litters** in a year. There are four to eight baby mice in each litter.

3

Raccoons have a black stripe on their faces that makes them look like masked robbers. Raccoons are very popular animals in North America, but no one should try to get too close to one. They have sharp teeth and can give a nasty bite.

The favourite homes of raccoons living in the country-side are hollow trees. When they live in towns and cities they live under sheds and even in the roofs of houses. Raccoons come out at night and look for things to eat. They like nuts and fruit, such as raspberries, cherries and plums. They also eat insects and steal birds' eggs. When they live in towns they often upset dustbins looking for scraps and steal food put out for birds. This makes them unpopular with some people.

Bats spend the day asleep and come out at night. Some kinds of bats sleep in houses and other buildings. These are European long-eared bats. They often live in the roofs of houses. Bats like to live in modern houses because they are warm and comfortable. The bats wake up in the evening and fly out when it is getting dark. They fly around outside the houses in search of insects to eat.

Fruit bats are large bats that live in warm countries. They eat fruit and flowers instead of catching insects. They are sometimes called flying foxes. These flying foxes live in Sydney, Australia. They come into gardens where there are fruit trees.

7

Brown rats live all over the world. They have been carried in ships even to small islands. They are pests because they eat our food and spread disease. They also attack and kill other animals, such as small birds. People are always trying to get rid of brown rats with traps and poison, but they are not very successful. There are still rats everywhere.

Baby rats can be born at any time of the year. There are usually between five and ten babies in a **litter**. Baby rats are blind and have no fur when they are born. When they are three weeks old they leave the nest and go for short walks with their mother. This helps them learn about the outside world. They discover what is good to eat and how to avoid danger. The father rat has nothing to do with the babies.

Badgers are European animals that come out only at night. Usually they will avoid being seen by people. Each family of badgers has a **burrow** called a **sett**. The badgers sleep during the day in a nest of dried grass at the bottom of the sett. They come out in the evening and often play together. Then they set off in search of food. Their favourite food is earthworms.

Some people like to see badgers in their gardens. They put food out for the badgers. Other people get upset when badgers knock dustbins over to search for scraps of food. Badgers also dig holes in lawns and flower-beds when they are looking for worms to eat.

Foxes are very common in some towns and cities. They become so tame that they can be seen even during the day. Usually they only come out at night. They come into gardens to steal scraps from dustbins and take food from birdtables. Some people are worried that foxes will kill cats. This does not happen very often. Cats are good at defending themselves.

Many people like hedgehogs in their gardens and put out bowls of milk for them. Hedgehogs usually eat worms, slugs and insects.

Hedgehogs live in Europe. They are covered with very sharp prickles called spines. When a hedgehog is frightened, it rolls into a ball and its spines stop animals attacking it. This dog is just sniffing the hedgehog.

Baby hedgehogs do not have spines when they are born. They grow a proper coat of spines when they are two weeks old. When the babies are four weeks old they go for walks with their mother.

Hedgehogs spend the winter asleep in a nest of dead leaves because they cannot find enough food in cold weather. This is called **hibernation**.

Cardinals are one of the many kinds of birds that come into gardens in North America. Cardinals are common birds there. They feed on birdtables in the winter and build their nests in bushes in summer.

At the end of summer swallows fly south to tropical countries where they spend the winter. They fly north again in the spring when the weather gets warmer and there are plenty of insects to eat. Swallows can catch insects in the air.

Swallows build their nests in barns and sheds that have wide windows or doors so the swallows can fly in and out.

15

House sparrows often live in cities and towns. They eat scraps of food that careless people have dropped. Some sparrows are so tame that they will take food from people's hands.

House sparrows once lived only in Africa. They spread into Europe and Asia thousands of years ago when people first grew crops. The sparrows liked to eat the corn. People have taken sparrows to other countries. One hundred years ago, sixteen sparrows were let go in New York. Now there are sparrows all over North America.

House sparrows build their nests in holes in buildings. The nests are untidy balls of grass with linings of feathers. Most birds leave their nests when the baby birds can fly, but house sparrows live in their nests all the year.

Starlings are common in towns and cities. They come into gardens and chase smaller birds from the food on birdtables. They also search for worms on the lawn.

Every evening starlings gather into large **flocks** and fly to the **roost** where they spend the night. They often roost on buildings in the middle of cities. Thousands of starlings gather on roofs and windowsills. They make a very loud noise until they go to sleep.

Starlings make their nests in holes in trees and buildings. The male sings outside and helps the female gather grass, sticks and leaves for the nest. When the babies have hatched both parents gather worms and insects for the baby starlings to eat.

Peregrines are rare birds but a few live in cities. Peregrines are called **birds of prey** because they catch and eat other birds, especially pigeons. Pigeons are very common in many cities so there is plenty of food for the peregrines.

City peregrines lay their eggs on window-ledges on high buildings. These places are like the ledges on cliffs where peregrines normally nest in the countryside.

Kestrels are another kind of bird of prey. They often live in towns. This one is nesting in a windowbox on someone's house. Kestrel's hunt mice and other small animals that live in long grass. They also catch small birds.

Frogs are called **amphibians** because they can live both on land and in the water. Toads and newts are also amphibians.

In the spring, frogs come into gardens with ponds to lay their eggs. The eggs of frogs are called **spawn**. Each egg has a coat of jelly. After three weeks the eggs hatch and tadpoles come out. Tadpoles have to live in water. During the summer the tadpoles slowly change into adult frogs.

Geckos are a kind of lizard that lives in hot countries. They often come into houses at night. People are happy to see geckos because they eat insects.

Geckos are amusing to watch because they can run up walls and across ceilings. Their feet have thousands of tiny suckers that will even stick to glass.

Index/Glossary

amphibian: an animal that spends part of its life in water and part on land. It usually lays its eggs in water. Frogs, toads, newts and salamanders are amphibians 23

badger 11
bats 7
  fruit 7
  long-eared 7
bird of prey: a bird that catches and eats animals. Eagles, hawks and falcons are birds of prey 21
brown rat 9
burrow: a hole dug by an animal for shelter 11

cardinal 15

flock: a group of birds or other animals that spend their time together 19
flying fox 7
fox 11
frog 23
fruit bat 7

gecko 23
hedgehog 13

hibernation: the winter sleep of some animals. They go to sleep in the autumn and hardly wake up at all until spring. Bats, hedgehogs, frogs and snakes hibernate 13
house mouse 3
house sparrow 16

kestrel 21

litter: a family of baby animals that were born at the same time. Cats, dogs, rats and mice have litters.
long-eared bat 7

peregrine 21

raccoon 5
roost: the place where birds rest and sleep. Sometimes many birds roost together 19

sett: the underground home of badgers 11
spawn: the eggs of amphibians. Each egg is covered in jelly 23
starling 19
swallow 15

tadpole 23